Between Then and Now

poems by

Terry Cox-Joseph

Finishing Line Press
Georgetown, Kentucky

Between Then and Now

Copyright © 2018 by Terry Cox-Joseph
ISBN 978-1-63534-767-8 First Edition
All rights reserved under International and Pan-American Copyright Conventions. No part of this book may be reproduced in any manner whatsoever without written permission from the publisher, except in the case of brief quotations embodied in critical articles and reviews.

ACKNOWLEDGMENTS

"Shaving," "Fragments" – *Sweetbay Review*
"Mistaken" – *Voices on the Wind*
"Ex Libris" – *Allegro*
"Dried Paint" – *Poet's Domain*
"Suburban Casualty" – *Poet's Domain*

Publisher: Leah Maines
Editor: Christen Kincaid
Cover Art: "Selene, Moon Goddess," acrylic, Terry Cox-Joseph
Author Photo: Christopher Joseph
Cover Design: Leah Huete

Printed in the USA on acid-free paper.
Order online: www.finishinglinepress.com
also available on amazon.com

Author inquiries and mail orders:
Finishing Line Press
P. O. Box 1626
Georgetown, Kentucky 40324
U. S. A.

Table of Contents

Mistaken 1
Ex Libris 2
Driving Lessons 3
Food for the Winter Soul 5
Penmanship 101 6
Worry Lines 7
Bonnie Lass 8
Shaving Dad 9
Coming Apart 10
Fragments 11
Volition 12
March On 13
Cousin on the Line 14
Between Then and Now, Darling 15
Spirit Chair 16
Transition 18
Portal 19
Dementia Art 20
Unbearable Admissions 21
The Scottish Terrier 23
Dried Paint 25
On the Cusp 26
Christmas Moon 28
Lawnmower Mornings 30
Suburban Casualty 31
Dwelling 32

Mistaken

I was Lolly that day—espresso eyes,
chestnut locks,
baby teeth like crooked pearls,
camellia cheeks.

Our loss unspeakable,
you couldn't bear
to tell—Great-Grandma
frail, propped

on pillows, secured
with aluminum rails.
I was your ghost to fill the void.
Shh. Don't talk.

If I were silent, I'd earn
an extra box of crayons.
I learned that just because

you're senile
doesn't mean you're stupid.
She knew.

"She's been sick," you repeated.
"That's why she looks   smaller."

Grandma was a lady.
She never argued.
Her brow furrowed.

Something was wrong—

very, very   wrong.

Ex Libris

Soft glow of lamplight, half past ten.
Nancy Drew at the window with a flashlight,
Misty running through Chincoteague with my heart.
The Call of the Wild, anything with a wolf.
Sleep on the edge of a book, just one more page.

Nancy Drew at the window with a flashlight.
Candy wrappers piled in wastebasket, knee highs
ready for school. Illustrated dust jackets hug
books stacked in pyramids on my maple desk,
rectangular math tossed beneath chair.

Candy wrappers piled in wastebasket, knee highs tight.
Books on my dresser, in my bookcase, on my bed.
Library only a twenty minute walk, better than glass-top
candy counter. My greedy hands—*The Black Stallion,
Jane Eyre, My Side of the Mountain.*

Books on my dresser, in my bookcase, on my bed.
And this, something different, *The Diary of Anne Frank.*
Half past ten, soft glow of lamplight. Dad over my shoulder,
plucking book from my grasp, first time, forbidden.
Too old. Distressing. Weighty. Another day.

And this, something different, *The Diary of Anne Frank.*
I argue, first time. *I'm thirteen. So was she.*
My case is strong, my grip tight. His relinquishes.
Mumbles. Regrets. Sleep deferred on the edge of a book,
just one more page. I live for the sum of pages.

Driving Lessons

I change lanes effortlessly, tires steady
on pavement, thirty five years'
experience beneath my belt.
"Who taught you this?" he asks,
before the light turns green.
"You did, Dad."
He laughs for the hundredth time,
slaps his thigh, adjusts the button
on his sport coat. "Well, I knew that,
just wanted to make sure. Fine job,
superior skill. You learned well."

Sixteen and shaky, I gripped the wheel
like a lifeline, shuddered below his shouts,
"Cut the wheel! Hard to the left! Shift!
Now—give it gas!"
Curves loomed like monsters,
freeway on-ramps,
black ice, ingress, egress, torque,
drag, gears etched into dreams.
He willed me to ride
the rusted Buick hard, his
glittering Cooper in fifth.

We divided his racing trophies between us—
five kids, five families, five states. He's
convinced that the nurses are maids who
do his laundry, polish his silver trophy cup.
Sometimes I watch the old film of him
spinning out on oil where he crashed
his favorite—the red MacLaren.
"I never drove a MacLaren," he insists.
"But that red car, now that car could *go*."

The light turns green. "Who taught you this?"
"You did, Dad." He laughs, slaps his thigh,
adjusts the button on his sport coat. "Well,
I knew that. But tell me," he adds, tone
warning that a driver will overtake me
on the curve, "have you been to any
of the other planets?"
"No," I say, thinking,
but you gave me the moon.

Food for the Winter Soul

On weekends, he settled into the indentation
that left no doubt as to whose plush gold chair

side-stepped the window. Curtain of newspaper
rested on stretched, crisply trousered legs

while snow crowded windowsills. Lamp shade
skirted a buttery circle of light, fresh baked pumpernickel

stacked on coffee table, wine red and woody.
He sipped between paragraphs, exhaled

between editorials. No caviar on this Westfalia loaf.
Thick, creamy butter smeared so thick it weighted

the already heavy slices, we cradled whole pieces
in our palms, opened wide to fill our bellies

against the chill. My siblings preferred WonderBread,
white and spongy like snow, no rich German

history of rye or medieval farming. Dad and I
dunked our pumpernickel in Mom's vegetable

beef soup, thick brown chunks tinted
with chocolate and coffee aromas,

strands of beef clinging to corners,
brown on brown. I still buy fresh baked

pumpernickel, search for elusive dark,
baked longest. Twenty-four hours is best,

time coaxed like a warm caress,
memories that rise like yeast.

Penmanship 101

You've still got a strong signature,
the nurse remarks, watching him
sign the ledger. Fighting

an index finger curled with arthritis,
his signature sashays
with the boldness of a judge, clarity

of a schoolteacher, finesse
of a Hollywood star.
He has always been
a decisive man,
determined.

Iconoclast, sign here.

Worry Lines

I ask how Dad's doing, if he still grumbles
about the home. A familiar tug in my chest
with my sister's staccato reply—he doesn't
answer the phone, she's on her way to check,
should never have given him
the keys   but he promised,
he was being so good,
he was adjusting,
he'd quit arguing
about the car.

Snap shut the cell phone, slam the lid on a casket.
This isn't the same. Mom was alone in her cancer,
everyone knew, but Dad could wipe out a family.

I retrieve her message from the tiny keypad
like a genie from a bottle.

Dad never left the building,
sat with a resident so young
she needn't color her hair.
He fails to notice her tremor,
her walker. He'd been good,
my sister said, as though
he were a small child.

Exhale, feel the saliva flow.
Chuckle. Woman's allure outweighs
freedom of a six-cylinder.

My glance
in the rearview mirror reveals
the crease between my brows.
I know my sister sees hers, too.

Bonnie Lass

*There will be a time in the not-so-distant
future where he won't recognize you.*

I've been warned. Nor'easter, slap
in the face,
though he never slapped me
all the years I grew up. In assisted living,
he surprises us with a girlfriend eighteen years
his junior. She doesn't notice his twisted thumb,
hunched shoulders—just the way he defers to her,
pours her wine first, reminisces about Dublin.

Her name is fleeting as the swallows that dart
through the loggia,
but he knows that behind that door
with the woven Irish wreath he'll find
that redhead who laughs at his jokes,
takes him by the arm, adjusts his chair at bingo.
I used to wonder how anyone could be
as forgiving as she, when my father blurted
again about her weight, hurt skimming her face.
But her smile returned as she offered,
*I don't remember
what you just said.*

Walking past her door, his happiness
is solid as Celtic stone
surrounded by ephemeral
autumn fog. It grants me hope
that when
he doesn't recognize me,
he'll still remember
my smile.

Shaving Dad

Steel and foam work a symbiosis
on his grizzled cheek. He pulls
the razor across the same patch twice,

thrice, now ten times, unaware that his
is the progress of the unknowing. Wizened
white hairs escape collar of his soft blue robe,

jowls sag with forgotten collagen
and muscle. My sister grasps the razor
in her long, slim fingers, smoothes his chin,

upper lip, jawline with precise strokes,
task so simple it breaks her heart,
not as much for love as loss.

If wishes were horses, Dad would
shave his own beard today. The bathroom
would echo with the clatter of hooves

and impatience, virility and purpose, Dad
first to grab the pommel, shove his boot in
the stirrup, hoist himself onto the saddle

and gallop alone into the past, singular figure
one with the stallion, plaque-ridden dendrites
and axons awhirl behind his determined steed.

Coming Apart

Can't stand to have his hair washed—cape snapped
around his neck, nylon crinkles exploding
against his eardrums to the ceiling
like the screech of jet engines,
spray of water needling his flesh.
Snip of scissors makes him cringe.

Moored in Leyte, he chewed ham sandwiches
deckside, bloated bodies beached beneath
his feet, then put five kids through
Catholic school under the shadow of
acid trips and Helter Skelter, raced
his 8-cylinder McLaren 200 miles an hour,
held his wife's thin hand
as the nurse adjusted her feeding tube.

My sister rubs his shoulders, barber homes in,
adjusts, whisks silver curls with a fluffy
round brush. Hairs whoosh the back
of his neck, flutter to the floor,
Dad's eyes roll,
he cries out,
mouth gaping,
      what,
why?

Fragments

I

I feed him chocolate,
broken squares with almond bits,
dark smudges smear my fingertips
poised above his lips.
I pop them into his opened mouth,
watch him chew, open, chew,
silently clamoring
for more.

II

He refused his shower again, rolled over,
yanked yellow blanket, turned his back
on the nurse. My promises lure him
to bathroom, one task at a time, divided
like chocolate. Blue trousers drop
to white tile. Warm water,
perfumed soap steam the mirror.

III

He sleeps on his side, away from broken hip.
Plumped pillow, oxycodone welcomed embrace.
Bright window across the room reveals reassuring
traffic that moves like electric current. Birch leaves
emerge lime green outside the windowsill. He opens
his eyes, follows cars' movement beyond the tree line,
roofline the same, and the same,
and just for a moment, all is well.

Volition

Red scar on your hip is calmer
today, holding tight
with new ball and socket,
rotation smooth, muscles secure.

Legs like pistons steady and sure,
90 years of practice hold true.
You're on your way, speeding
bullet, Superman from comic
book days, focused, short trip
to the bathroom
on your own,
on your own, again.

March On

Roosevelt couldn't have known
that his words would presage your demise,
years beyond others' lifespans. You wander

into apartments not yours, slap
nurses who approach too quickly,
fear doctor's stethoscope, elevator shaft,

that leather chair over there, monsters all.
Bathed in sweat, arms flail, fists clench,
fear of the unknown, life shrouded

with amorphous beginnings,
shredded context, fear of fear itself,
like that famous inaugural speech,

your journey an abyss. Who would know
that an eggroll could cause such terror,
cradled in daughter's fingers, words

caressing air, floating to the ceiling in mist
of hieroglyphics. You used to eat Chinese
once a week, gave Mom a break from

hot stove, all those kids, ginger, sweet and sour
permeating white shutters and rooster curtains,
relaxing tense shoulders, weary legs.

You used to march with purpose,
familiar fatigues, unprepared for how right
your president was, how prophetic.

Cousin on the Line

Phone against my ear, I ask how she's feeling, but—
too late—I can tell by the breathy squeal of her *hello*
it's a down day and wonder if I can fake a bad connection.
Awake all night, pain shooting up her tailbone, alligator
jaws. I know what she means, how she uses her thumb
and fingers to motion out the pinches, tap-snap-snip.
Each day the same, Oxy perpetuating Sisyphean cycle
of nerve loops. Too late. She refused PT. No more
rehearsals. Cousin insists that the home is short-staffed,
one of the nurses whispered, *don't tell,* only one on the
unit. Surely, nurse should be assigned to her and her only—
remember, *Darling,* she had her own dressing room off-stage,
rap-tap, five minutes till showtime. Her pitch rises, pinging
off fiber optics like an electric shock, zam-slap-slamming
my heart until ribs vibrate. Didn't get her Percocet all night,
don't they care? And no Tramadol, nothingnothingnothing
for the pain, no one to help her, no one to answer the call
bell, she will leave if it's going to be like this, and I wonder
if they really are short-staffed, or if a nurse pocketed the meds,
or my cousin forgot, awakened from sleep for a sleeping pill
like a Jack Benny routine, diagnosis scribbled on a chart that
no one reads. I will never know unless I stop by after lunch
to count pills at nurses station, run my finger down the
printout, number the days, verify missing meds, insist
they're stolen, call an emergency meeting, fire the staff,
file a lawsuit, set a court date, fend off reporters. An hour
later opium derivatives diffuse their glow through her
bloodstream. She calls, laughs, asks me to remind her
when her cat goes to the vet for a checkup.

Between Then and Now, Darling

Born a charmer, burst from
        mother's womb that day,   gala
affair, you slid into doctor's hands
in ballet slippers, brown eyes
bedeviled and needy. Your parents
        encouraged precocity and sex appeal
to counteract Victorian corseting.
You left home too early, ignored   gossip,
danced your way through Reno
        when dancing was real and voices
weren't lip-synched.
Do you ever wonder what it would have
been like if you'd stayed home, learned
        calculus? Now, eight-by-ten   glossies
elbow one another from yellowed
        albums—thank God you wrote notes,
saved playbills. You would do it all again.
Even the loss. Overslept tryouts, roles unread.
Would that you stayed on proper medication.
        You nibbled supporting roles,   gulped
gimlets, withered to a numbered extra.
        Callbacks dwindled. You fell to your
finale offstage, dogs underfoot, tailbone
fractured along with rehearsals. PT was Oxy
with a merlot chaser. Re-runs in black-and-white,
        focus on the extra-long   gloves
and cleavage. You've forgotten
the subject. Blame someone.
Have a chocolate. Nurse brings   Gabapentin.
        Here, take a seat—extra soft cushion.
Ready the script. Raise the lights.
        Tell me a story.

Spirit Chair

I.

Terrified—you shouted on the phone—
friend forced you through icy midnight shadows,
brownstone across Seventy-fifth a prison,
despite same bedspread, familiar books. What
happened to your friends, how did your bed
get there? Yet you knew to call me.

Of course you walked there—you've been walking
since hospital. No broken coccyx, searing neuropathy
torture 'til dawn. Never mind that he'd just helped
you to the bathroom. Never mind that nameless
doctor who took cash from your handyman, sent him
back to you with more oxycodone *just that once*.

II.

Great-grandmother rocked you—*lullaby, and goodnight*—
rich brown mahogany, seat worn bare, gentle sway
on braided rug. You grew into ponytails and bobby socks.
She slipped you movie tickets. Ambitious eaglet, you fled
small town, supplanted her rocker with adrenaline,
applause, midnight martinis. New York, New York!

III.

You shipped me great-grandmother's rocker.
Don't refinish, you warned. *It will lose its spirit.*
Creek of runners by my living room window.
Worn pegs, splintered wood not meant to last
a hundred years languish on garage cement, scattered.

Terrified, you wept, *like pieces of me are breaking off,*
floating around. I coo over the phone. Nurse gives a pill.
In the cold garage, I pick up your pieces—
worn arm, stained spindles, scraped runner—
carry them into the house.

Transition

Your peach apartment a prison,
color swatches too numerous, pillows fluffed
out of a catalog, doors open to garden path,
birdfeeders, pink azaleas, crimson Japanese maples.
Purse overflows with Hersheys, shelves burst

with Sherlock Holmes and Jane Austen. Rose
chintz cascades over wingback. Yet grief
permeates each raindrop, clouds turn your heart.
Never enough pain pills to erase Beloved's
head on your shoulder in hospital. His ring

swivels on your finger, three sizes too big
from weight that evaporates from your bones.
You refuse your walker, envision
ice skating, dancing just around the corner,
old friends picking you up, never mind

they moved to the suburbs years ago. I stripped
urine-soaked sheets, called your landlord, mailed
checks—no eviction, that month. No proper goodbyes,
but it was your idea to live near family. I drove you
to surgery, weaned you off opiates, forced you—

ha!—forced you to shop at Macy's,
sip wine at French cafés. Yet my phone
rings your plea fifteen times a day.
Pain leaps from the head-set like Pandora's box,
touch of a button silences, but it's too late.

You follow me everywhere.

Portal

She stares. Again. Gazes beyond
my shoulder until phantom fingers tingle
back of my neck. My cousin beckons
a woman behind me, bids her to sit.
I know this vacancy is occupied.

Cousin's mind and a beige
hospital curtain.
Yet I turn.
This being has come only
to visit. This time.
Chat, stopover, first call.

My cousin was always indecisive.
Why should Death be different?

No names. They come and go.
Friends, strangers, queens and kings,
cats and dogs share transition, amorphous
travel. Cousin's fingers knead blankets,
purposeless movements that occupy
translucent hands, provide sustenance
for nerve endings seeking direction.

"Heeere Whiskers!"
She reaches for my hair. Gently,
her too-long fingernails scratch
my scalp, soothe me, her beloved.

I am cat, I am neighbor, I am friend.
I am the last reality, fragile link
between this world and

next.

Dementia Art

Train train train
she shouts from her wheelchair.
Toot toot toot
why why why
go away go away go away.

I focus on buttery smooth white paint,
strokes to highlight clouds, solidify
two-dimensional fence, add Hooker's green
to my palette—leaves, stalks, stems, shadows.

Looks looks looks
White white white
Clouds clouds clouds.

I turn to smile at wheelchair woman.
She stares at the door I disguise, now sated,
a child watching my performance. Air inflates
with Prussian blue, loaded brush drips onto drop cloth.

Not not not
Go go go
End end end.

She veers, her words like wild geese
honking farewell across the sky.
Conflagration, cacophony, then
distant voices rising
and fading on the wind.

This is the end, the way out,
colored by my hand, no way out
beyond a fence with no gate,
sky without horizon.

Unbearable Admissions

And now, it's my turn. I hold
Cousin's hand, bird bones
arching heavenward, dodge
her clouded eyes, my lies
of omission piled
like unread books.

First, my granddaughter,
out-of-wedlock, as they
called it Back When. Teen
son high with buddies, never
stopped by Labor and Delivery.
Now, smitten with another love,
court-ordered payments
substitute for play-dates.
"He's fine," I smile.

Then, my brother's cancer,
rare as solar eclipse, his treatments
calculated risks. He, our parents'
trophy. Their forever absence a
blessing now—it would have
shattered them, like Great-Grandma.
"He's busy,"
I say, true enough.

Your brother, gone since '91,
found at the kitchen table, frozen.
Like he'd sat down to Kellogg's.
"Dial his number," you say,
simple as asking the Operator.
"When I get home," I promise,
wiping lies from my lips
with a sleeve.

I strain with the burden of stories
untold. "She couldn't bear to hear,"
they explained years later.
"It would have broken her." I promise
myself a glass of wine if I'm quiet,
new book if I'm good.

The Scottish Terrier

Until his jaws bored through
the bridge of my nose, blood
veiled my eyes, poured onto

our favorite rug, clogged
my throat till I gagged,
I never realized how tenuous

life is, like walking through
a cloud when the bottom falls out.
Air. Just air. The only thing that ever

held me up. Vise of gleaming, white
incisors, my life seized. His rage stripped
my universe, every painting, poem,

kiss halted in crunch of bone and cartilage.
Every meal seasoned, every seatbelt
snapped in satisfaction obliterated

in that shivering grip. All moments attract
this moment like a magnet, all life
congeals into this blood.

Feel the dark stairs with the soles of your heart.
Listen to the siren at the door with ears left intact.
Trust the stranger who covers your face

leaving just enough light to pull the threads
of your life back together, stanch the flow
of precious iron and nutrients, piece together

just enough of you to move through space,
to cling to another's arm wondering
if this time,

you'll both go down,
the sidewalk beneath nothing more
than ephemeral moisture, trust

a skill that grows one
fragile
molecule
at a time.

Dried Paint

Hush, child, while the stars dance
overhead, crickets sing you to sleep,
nightlight guides my path down the hall
to my studio. There is still time for painting.

Stop your shouting, child. Sing, don't shriek.
Throw balls, not blocks.
Drink this prepackaged juice,
busy yourself with these cartoons
while I fling purple and green on this still life.

Tell your friends to stop calling so late.
Take your long legs off the coffee table, child.
Clock hands stretch toward tomorrow,
shrill peal of phone agitates.
The pigment of my spirit will not flow
while pandemonium possesses my easel.

I once dreamed I was an artist
who yearned to create inspiration from nothing,
but my canvas was never blank.
It was painted with the soft pat-pat
of tiny steps in footie pajamas,
spilled red juice, walls scribbled with green crayon,

homework papers crumpled between sofa cushions,
small bodies bursting into adolescence like red and yellow
parrot tulips forcing their way through blue ice,
a head study in charcoal, stranger
whose tires crunch the gravel driveway
in pursuit of a tree-lined campus.

My two dimensional pieces stretched flat,
I strain to siphon the spirit of life from a tube of paint
as though it will recreate the vision
I lost when life seized control of my brush.

On the Cusp

I.   *Overcrowding*

I have read that madness does not always howl—
sometimes it is a small voice inside your head,
asking, is there room for one more? Mine does
not ask. It stabs my cerebellum, yanks chunks of
ventricles, bores through my amygdala. Apuleius'
Psyche had to earn back her husband. I fight for
my mind. It's not that I never appreciated my
sanity, just that I never realized how life could
obliterate spirit. I reveal no bruised flesh for
Exhibit A, merely pervasive osmosis that swarms
synapses, reduces gray matter to puddled proteins.

II.   *Desolation*

I don't think its origin was my mind. It first gnawed
on my heart, digested it whole. Insatiable, it invaded
my judgment, by degrees inserting rage and frustration,
silencing my attempted antidotes: strains of Bach and
Paganini, strokes of vermillion and cobalt on canvas,
scent of hyacinth. I know why madness howls, gripping
barred windows in cold hospital corridors where shrieks
pelt cracked linoleum. It howls to drown that small,
insistent voice in my head that reminds me that I was
once visionary. It whispers *come back, come back.*
But there is nothing to come back to.

III.   Genesis

Sliver of light ribbons the horizon, fragment of poem.
Dance of assonance, counsel of rhythm. Synapses
swell like watered roses. Capricious changeling,
small voice whispers *come back*, proffers alluring
imagery, similes. Stars flicker encouragement.
Skipjacks murmur metaphors. Dare I trust? Words
cascade, coalesce into substance and syntax. Behold—
an open heart, vibrant verses, molded form and meter.
Something to come back to.

Christmas Moon

What I see is a breathtaking digital image
of a full moon on Christmas,
first in thirty years
but what I think
is that hundreds of cell phones have been
purchased at Walmarts in Missouri
with cash, by men whose accents
alarm the clerks who call the FBI.

What I see are red and green ribbons
and dancing reindeer
but what I think
is that this may be the last holiday
with my family before another
9/11 splinters our world, collision
of Mohammed's birthday on the eve
of Christmas, holiday forever tainted.

What I see is a mishmash of stockings,
hung on nails I dared tap into the mantelpiece,
gold thread and red velvet fastened
near whimsical curled elf toe and bells,
and child's glitter scrawl on 1960's vestige
but what I think
is that my son most likely won't come home,
he'll be stoned under a stranger's tree.

What I see are neighbors' icicle lights
dancing on roof edges, inflated snowmen
and Grinches communing on lawns
but what I think
is that I prefer to walk the boat path,
light filtered through bare dogwoods
and hollies, dogs beside me, sniffing ferns
and deer tracks.

Terry Cox-Joseph is a member of the Poetry Society of Virginia and is a former newspaper reporter and editor. From 1994-2004 she was the coordinator for the annual Christopher Newport University Writers' Conference and Contest. An award-winning poet, she has been published in *Northern Virginia Review, Allegro, Chiron Review, The Blotter, Avocet,* and *Red River Review,* among others. She displays and sells her watercolors, acrylics and oils at Blue Skies Gallery in Hampton, Virginia. Her children, pets and the waterfront provide a constant resource for her writing and art.

www.ingramcontent.com/pod-product-compliance
Lightning Source LLC
LaVergne TN
LVHW041506070426
835507LV00012B/1358